Autogeography

Autogeography

Poems

Reginald Harris

NORTHWESTERN UNIVERSITY PRESS

EVANSTON, ILLINOIS

Northwestern University Press
www.nupress.northwestern.edu

Printed in the United States of America

10   9   8   7   6   5   4   3   2   1

Library of Congress Cataloging-in-Publication Data
Harris, Reginald, 1960–
    Autogeography : poems / Reginald Harris.
      p. cm.
    ISBN 978-0-8101-2915-3 (pbk. : alk. paper)
    I. Title.
    PS3608.A78327A94 2013
    811.6—dc23

                                    2012049554

For

Edna Harris
(1986–2000)

Melvin Harris
(1903–2007)

Voyagers

The city seems a mirage, dishonest
with constant movement, or so shy
it flattens into image, then shimmers.
Seeing is strange! Free of the dark,
sharp spots of color float, shapes wave,
bounce—an endless cacophony of surfaces.
You're vulnerable, trying to fashion it all
into a tapestry that means *this I know.*

—Sharan Strange, "First Sight," in *Ash* (2001)

CONTENTS

ACKNOWLEDGMENTS

Many thanks to the editors of the following journals in which many of these poems appeared, at times in slightly different form:

Attic: "Who I Think You Are"

Baltimore Review: "Magicians"

5 AM: "Atlantic City"

Gargoyle: "Approaching Baltimore"

Kweli Journal: "Reunion"

La Petite Zine: "While the Quartet Plays 'Body and Soul' "

Little Patuxent Review: "Among the Players"

Loch Raven Review: "Out of Town"

Margie: The American Journal of Poetry: "Gospel"

MELUS Journal: "Travel Journal"

Milk Magazine: "Nom de Plume"

Obsidian III: "Bluetopia" and "Song for My Father"

Pebble Lake Review: "*Baltimore Uproar* by Romare Bearden"

Poetry Midwest: "Deya"

Segue: "Poem Based on a Line by Forman"

Smartish Pace: "The Poets at the Ball Game"

Sou'wester: "Colonnade Shop, Havana" and "Packing"

suspect thoughts: "Trailer Park Self-Portrait"

WarpLand: A Journal of Black Literature and Ideas: "Crying Man with Broom" and "The Man with My Name"

WordWrights Magazine: "On the Road"

Xavier Review: "Eastside Alphabetics," "The Lost Boys: A Requiem," and "What Are You?"

✧

Thanks also to the editors of the following anthologies in which poems appeared:

Cave Canem II: 1997 Anthology (New York: Cave Canem Foundation, 1997): "The Poet Behind the Wheel"

Cave Canem V: 2000 Anthology (New York: Cave Canem Foundation, 2000): "Sunday Brunch"

Poems Against War: Bending Toward Justice—An Anthology, edited by Gregg Mosson (Shelbyville, Ky.: Wasteland Press, 2010): "Marvin Gaye Sings 'The Star-Spangled Banner'"

Role Call: A Generational Anthology of Social and Political Black Literature and Art, edited by Tony Medina, Samiya Bashir, and Quraysh Ali Lansana (Chicago: Third World Press, 2002): "New Rules of the Road"

September Eleven: Maryland Voices, edited by Rus VanWestervelt (Baltimore: Posner Press, 2002): "The City Without You"

Voices Rising: Celebrating 20 Years of Black Lesbian, Gay, Bisexual and Transgender Writing, edited by G. Winston James (Washington, D.C.: RedBone Press, 2007): "Notes Toward a Poem About Love"

War Diaries, edited by Tisa Bryant and Ernest Hardy (Los Angeles: Institute for Gay Men's Health, 2009): "*Cuerpo de hombre,*" "Dream of My Cousin's Wedding," and "Sonnet: LeatherBoy"

Audio versions of "Approaching Baltimore" and "Eastside Alphabetics" appear on *From the Fishouse* (www.fishousepoems.org).

"On the Road" also appears in *The Ringing Ear: Black Poets Lean South,* edited by Nikky Finney (Athens: University of Georgia Press, 2007). Some lines in the poem are sampled from "Dawn Revisited" by Rita Dove.

All lines in "The Spinning Song" are titles of compositions by Herbie Nichols (1919–1963).

"Trailer Park Self-Portrait" also appears in *Best Gay Poetry 2008,* edited by Lawrence Schimel (Maple Shade, N.J.: Lethe Press, 2009).

✵

I am grateful beyond words to Cave Canem, Janice Harrington, and Parneshia Jones for the amazing gift of selecting my manuscript for the Cave Canem Northwestern University Press Poetry Prize. Many, many thanks to the many friends who looked at various versions of this manuscript over the years: Samiya Bashir, Sharon Bridgforth, Jericho Brown, Linda Joy Burke, Hayes Davis, Teri Cross Davis, Steven G. Fullwood, Duriel Harris, Sean Hill, Tyehimba Jess, John Keene, Nicole McFarlane, David Mills, Lisa Moore, Evie Shockley, Kevin Simmonds, Marvin K. White, and L. Lamar Wilson.

Autogeography

The Poet Behind the Wheel

is dangerous. Juggling pad, pen,
steering column, each traffic light
brings forth a line, every *Yield* a different
turn of phrase. The speedometer

counts out syllable, not speed,
and directions come apart under his fingers.
Maps lose their meaning Right? Second
left?   Gas station?—
Only words, playing cards to be reshuffled later.

Do not get caught behind him:
        He drives slowly, leads followers astray.
Do not honk your horn:
        It reminds him of Purcell, Armstrong, the Walls of Jericho.

Do NOT let him drive you:
        Buckle up and hours later
        who knows where you'll arrive.

Approaching Baltimore

Magic City, Magic City, ya'll
Got that Magic City, Magic City, ya'll

. . . the imploded high-rise, empty
houses rows of busted teeth in
a crooked smile. Trash-filled corner
lots. Ghetto Chinese, yat gaw mein
with ketchup, with or without egg.
Six wings and fries. Black-clad homeboys
swimming down the block, calling
"loose ones, loose ones" (*Magic City, Magic City, ya'll*) as they
pull up sagging baggies, bop away: No

easy way into this ugly beauty, once
elegant lady in a tattered dress (*Magic City, Magic City, ya'll*). No
sweeping vistas from any approach—The highway
curves and there: a tangle of overpasses,
bombed out streets behind a scrim of
abandoned steel mills and auto plants,
unused loading docks. (*Magic!*)

Learn to live with, love, imperfection,
the close enough to right, whatever
will make do (*Magic City, Magic City, ya'll*). Handsome men with
knife scars across the face, exhausted
women dragging three tattered children
down the street. What happens to a dream

4

transferred, outsourced, shuttered, boarded
up? Which ways take you in, and which way out? And what grows there?

Magic City, Magic City, ya'll   *Got that Magic City, Magic City, ya'll*

Eastside Alphabetics

Apostolic   Beat down   Chicken box
     Down low   E-dealer   Five-O car
         Gospel hip-hop   Ice cream jones

Kenya, Kendra,
     Keyshawn, Ko-Ko   Ko-rean's
         Laun-dro-mat

Methadone nod out
     Noontime   Old school   Preschool
         Quit school

Queen Ray's
     Quick Mart   4-Real Hair   Shock
         Trauma   SUV

Wheelchair wigger
     Whiteboy wannabes
         "XXLs right here, y'all"
                 ! Zoom !

Crying Man with Broom

He's on his way to his third job of the day,
cleaning out the overheated storeroom. Forced
to move, he's just swept the muck of the previous
tenant's life from his cramped apartment. Perhaps

it's for the friend who's finally dropped the crystal
candy dish everyone but him mistakes for an ashtray,
in need of more than yesterday's newspaper to pick up
the tiny pieces. Old and battered, it is the broom

his youngest daughter jumped over on her wedding day;
her daughter needs it now to make her leap. Or is it his
own—marriage long since over—broom the only relic of
his former life. And those aren't tears but sweat you see

coursing down his cheeks. He hasn't cried in years. The broom?
useless, an antique, he's on his way to drop it in the trash.

Gospel

spills out from the headphones
to hum low in her throat

so full, the music over-
flows from her mouth

onto the crowded bus
bursts from her as she leaves

to fill the morning streets
with song.

Commuters murmur, nudge each
other, laugh at her departure,

return to silence, morning
papers, their own thoughts.

Contemplate
a God-shaped echo in the air.

Sonnet: LeatherBoy

Many's the time I've seen his mocha-
colored back enlaced with scars, stripes,
crisscrossed with the interlocking hash
marks of his last partner's whip, emblems
of a night's hard play, the joys of submission
and intensity cascading down from shoulder
blade to the still glowing caramel of his plump
firm ass.

Moving through the darkened
bar, the crowd parts, stares in awe
at his proud display, desire, lust, and envy
flowing in his broad-smiling wake,
our eyes a second licking, soothing balm,
a salve to cool down his still-hot flesh,
caresses his luscious, passion-tattooed skin.

Fanaticism? No. Writing is exciting
and baseball is like writing.
You can never tell with either
how it will go
or what you will do . . .

—Marianne Moore, "Baseball and Writing" (1961)

The Poets at the Ball Game

are not used to such good seats:
behind third base, a perfect view,
outfield grass as green as Lorca's *Verde*
que te quiero verde. They feel a bit like
Miss Moore, honored by the Yankees in '68
to toss out the first pitch,

dream of "Poetry Day at the Park":
a personalized sonnet for the first
one hundred fans and free haiku for kids.
The crowd raps out rhythms with minibats,
signed by the poet laureate, count iambs
during the caesura of the seventh inning stretch,
recite heroic couplets for the hitter who launches

a long fly beyond the upper deck, filled
with visiting midshipmen, white uniforms a blur.
They cheer with the sound of frothing waves,
a thousand cranes in flight.
A forest of blank pages tossed aloft.

Baltimore Orioles vs. Tampa Bay Devil Rays
Camden Yards, Baltimore, Maryland
August 9, 2005

Baltimore Uproar by Romare Bearden
Upton/Avenue Market Metro Station, Baltimore, Maryland

Get off here. This is a story you've
been told: these streets before the trash,
the rats, the crackheads nodding to ghost
music. That past a distant gleam of notes,
sound magicians dreaming, rising
from these streets: diminutive
personifications of the beat, rhythm
made compact flesh; flamboyant
fly-brimmed hipsters high on Hi de Ho,
lexicographers of jive; and Our Dark Lady,
transformed from turning tricks to
trickster by the music, through her songs.

From The Avenue to the after-hours you
could hear it in the changes, the shift from
working day to glittering night. Shattering
twists of phrase calling out, the turn of a gloved
hand sheathed in silver from fingertip to elbow
to hide the tracks beneath. Rising from the
platform, the scent of gardenias is in the train's
retreating roar, leaving departing commuters
in spangled shards of sound. These multicolored stones
are her petals, a frozen music always calling,
calling back, urging on—*Rise up. Get off here. Rise*
up

Reunion

Basquiat's on the back steps with my niece
helping her to draw a picture of us all,
tossing back gray dreadlocks as they fall
into his eyes. My sister argues politics

with Martin and Coretta in the backyard
over ribs—Romare Bearden's cooking—
Malcolm puts his two cents in between

bites of peas and rice. My grandfather
flirts with Billie as they remember the old
days on The Avenue in West Baltimore. Pres
brushes off his porkpie hat and stands, offers

to get my grandmother something from
the dessert table. She declines, full from her
second helping of Duke Ellington's homemade

apple pie. Essex and Joe Beam line dance with
Audre and Pat Parker while Assotto Saint,
Melvin Dixon, and my partner critique
from the picnic table off to one side.

Shamefaced, my father shows up late,
as always, with Charlie Parker and Bud Powell in tow.
Where've you-all been? my mother asks.
She gets a kiss and sheepish grin, but no reply.

Song for My Father
North Carolina, I-85, 4 A.M.

We turn up the same tunes
        on the radio   nod to the same beats
            scat the solos   wake the sleeping van
               with our duet

Music is our only language   Words
        do not pass as easily as notes
           transformed to understanding

We speak in phrases   trade silences
        and fours   wait for another song
           we both know   our favorite soloists
             to begin before we find agreement

A way to communicate
        something to connect us
           in the dark

While the Quartet Plays "Body and Soul"

Louie's Bookstore Café, Baltimore, Maryland, 1998

A man strums his lover's back like a guitar
    My heart is sad and lonely
        Conversations slide to whispers, end
            For you I sigh, for you dear only

            My heart is sad and lonely
                All heads nod, familiar with the tune
                    For you I sigh, for you dear only
                        Ringed fingers splay across a dark-sleeved arm

                        All heads nod familiar with the tune
                        You know I'm yours for just the taking
                Ringed fingers play across a dark-sleeved arm
                I'm all for you, body and soul

    You know I'm yours for just the taking
Welcome whiskey's fever in the throat
    I'm all for you, body and soul
Behind us someone whispers

Whiskey's a welcome fever in the throat
    I can't believe it, it's hard to conceive it
        Behind us someone whispers
            Are you pretending, it looks like the ending

        I can't believe it, it's hard to conceive it
            Evening's end plucks the skin like strings
                Are you pretending, it looks like the ending
                    Moving through the changes on a mission

Evening's end plucks the skin like strings
My life a wreck you're making
Moving through the changes on a mission
I spend my days in longing

My life a wreck you're making
In conversation about the measure of the days
I spend my days in longing
History in the repeats, their destination

a conversation about the measure of their days
Why haven't you seen it?
History is the repeats, the destination
I'm all for you, body and soul

Why haven't you seen it?
Conversations slide to whispers, end
I'm all for you, body and soul
A man strums his lover's back like a guitar.

My People

Turn the corner and there
THEY are, *Loud <u>and</u> Wrong,*
my grandmother says, head
already in mid-shake. *Used to be*
a good neighborhood too,
my grandfather adds, gripping
the steering wheel, unimpressed
by these low-rent others moving
in, blurring the red lines
separating white from black
casting dark shadows
on their West Side dreams.

Your people—No, YOUR
People. They bounce responsibility
for the stoop sitters and boom boxes,
chitterlings, bright polyester and Afro
Sheen back and forth between them

their words
flying over me
looking out
from the back-
seat at my face
in the mirrored
glass

The Star

Her closet is a universe
made for trying on
the brightly colored dresses,
a standing field of flowers
wider than the cramped stamp
of dirt behind the house.

Ignored every day starched white,
reached back into a past
still laced with big band music,
rationed cigarettes, Chanel No. 5,

Stepped into shoes and grew to
adolescence, the *clock clock clock*
of heels Time racing down the hall
to when he too would be tall, cool,
desirable—an adult—just like
Lena Horne.

> How could they not love him as
> he made his grand entrance, posed,
> placed a trembling hand on narrow hip,
>
> waited breathlessly, sure of their applause?

Dream of My Cousin's Wedding

We walk down the aisle together, he and I,
holding hands, shaking with held-in giggles:
too serious at thirteen, I am the man atop
the wedding cake come alive with blown-out
Afro and clip-on tie beside a cloud of gauze
and lace, my cousin, billowing, veil hiding
the thin hairs of his first mustache.

No one is surprised. All seem comfortable with
our mocking, pray this Tom Thumb dress-up
and pretend will purge us of the thing they fear,
both of us too quiet, different, strange—they have
suspicions, other names lying in wait to hang
on our thin shoulders if we do not reform, repent,
"grow out of it."

High on Communion wine transformed
into grape juice, we race to fly out of this
church, those clothes, that small town,
into cities, adulthood, our true names.
Seal our vows of escape with a stolen kiss.

The Lost Boys: A Requiem

Ricky who moved away when I was three
Jamie killed in a hit and run, aged 10
Wayne—fell from a project window, age 14
Keith—fell off a bridge at 17 (or was he pushed?)

Tee-Tee, Bam-Bam, Walter, Little Man
        Shot in a drive-by over money by
Black Charles, and Jeep
        Shot by Tee's cousin the following week

Jackie took him-
        self out with a gun

Butch who introduced me to my lover
        dead of AIDS, his lover
Jayson waited a whole month
        to follow

William lost to AIDS
Essex lost to AIDS
Joseph lost to AIDS
Tony lost to AIDS

Melvin whom I loved
        but never met
Kenny, fiercest young boy on the block—
        Everyone called him "faggot" from age 10

Andre behind bars
Michael behind bars
Emmett behind bars
Lennie behind bars

David and his stunning white fur coat
        disappeared after his mother's funeral
Stevie who saw "Police Line—Do Not Cross"
        could not resist

Baby Johnny, christened, dead in 30 days

Tony on crack
        Big K on crack
                Patrick on crack
                        Willie on crack

The Iron Man across the street
        did PCP
Keyshawn inhaled fire from freebase while
        brother Kevin did the White Girl
                and brother Kelvin took the Boy

Frankie swimming in a bottle, MD 20/20
Jerome in Johnny Walker Red
Ernest in a 40
Tommy in whatever he can get

Joe, not dead, only resting
Nathan, not lost, just gone
Troy, not gone, just not here
Richie—just—

Notes Toward a Poem About Love

Remember:
    The long trip back from the Carolinas—
        How he looked, smooth in silhouette   dozing.

You drove 80 miles an hour from Durham to D.C.
    Through rain-slicked, receding South
        Deep in a groove, desperate for return   for shared, familiar bed;

      Or earlier   the night before   the downtown Charlotte club—

How, even dressed in "b-boy hoodlum mode"
    He was glorious, shone   a beacon in the smoky dark
        New Man in Town, undressed by the eyes of Sunday regulars

Confused by this bastard busting their games
                The half-seen Other he leaves with;

      Or later even: Picture the future, next week, tomorrow—

He strides in from work   tired   complaining
    Of new madnesses   then winks
        Changes for his late night rituals

On the phone, he laughs at a joke and his gaze turns
                Ablaze with anticipated retelling.

Then forget:
    Think of Lack   The Absence of that Presence
        A world without memory   the otherwise dull moments

        Stop.   Think (*for once*).
Meditate.   Slowly begin to write.

Who I Think You Are

Forbidden fruit and the scent of pine   Familiar shirt
    contoured to fit my body   Shining armor, newly minted
       dime   An Age of Reason after long Dark Night

Perfect timing   Scheduled trains pulling into
    stations   Four-lane highways rain-washed and clean
       of traffic   Steady bridges over roiling waters

Budding rose and sturdy redwood tree   Apples and brown
    sugar on the tongue   Fresh baked bread   A finger pointing north
      The steady rower   Full moon and beating heart   Quiet *Welcome Home*

Atlantic City

Last time with my partner and his
coworkers: We stopped at Cowtown to buy
supposed bargains, kitschy gifts, before continuing
to Bally's, Caesar's, one of the Trumps,
pockets full of coins and bills, dreams
of quick-gotten riches filling our heads.

The first time with my parents,
before casinos, the city even then lost in
nostalgia for the '40s, the '30s,
the clubs that used to line the strip,
the weekends off from cleaning summerhouses
filled with juke joints, picnics on the beach,
Elks' parades and music, Louis Jordan, or Cab
Calloway singing *Hi de Ho* down the boardwalk.

In a fever, staring at the hotel's teenaged
lifeguard, quietly searching the bodies of men
gathered at New York Avenue (*Someone
had to tell me, how else did I know?*)
looking for a guidebook to who I knew I was becoming.

Briefly, with a long-distance lover
after hours in the car
driving away, not toward,
concentrating on the road, pointing
at the gray crawling ocean, our mouths filled
with saltwater taffy instead of words
        pain
loss   *betrayal*
               the end of something

Accidentally overnight in a cheap motel,
lodgings for the busted or by-the-hour whores,
the useless air conditioner rattling through the night
louder than the trucks out on the highway as we collapsed,
exhausted on the bed—then made love
anyway, thinking it expected by the room, needing
the reassurance of our touch to let us know
our lives were not as crapped out as those
who'd been there before us.

His eyes catch mine across the noisy
room. He smiles, jiggles a plastic cup
quarter full of change. I shrug, holding out a
fistful of coins.

Around us lights flash, bells ring and burr.
Nickels, dimes, silver
dollars rattle into metal pans.
Beside me someone calls out,

Jackpot!

Cuerpo de hombre

The waiter's ass sways like a cypress
in the breeze as he carries lunch trays
up a flight of stairs. Reed slim and dark

rich loam from the Carolinas, he's not
my type anymore: I've outgrown
young men like that, filled out to appreciate
thickness, density, weight: men with legs

like tree trunks, ripe apple full biceps
a temptation waiting to be eaten,
chests like grassy savannahs, wild plains
overrun with slightly graying hair.
But sometimes a breeze from my youth comes up

envelops me with the scent of discarded skin,
the men I've left behind, hypnotizes with
a sway and gentle shake, leaves my mouth
watering, tongue babbling like a sylvan brook.

The Man with My Name

Lives in another town.
Was born without
a pebble in his shoe.
Went straight home from
school. Did not get into
fights. Never ran.

Obeys speed limits, traffic lights,
DO NOT ENTER signs. Has never
been pulled over by police.
Married, fathered three. Moved to
the suburbs. Has every smooth
jazz album ever made.

Keeps his hair cut short. Promptly
answers mail. Returns
every phone call the same day.
Has never seen the Southern Cross,
or cried beneath the midnight sun.
Remembers names. His mother's face.

Plays baseball, basketball,
golf—for business reasons.
Loves talk radio. Laughs
at faggot jokes. Undresses
women in the office with his eyes.
Is an early riser. Still can't dance.

Stays in touch with college,
high school friends. Doesn't mind
he is the only black they know.

Works out. Eats his vegetables,
cleans his plate. Never chased
a penguin, startled a muskrat,

or kissed a man.
Always listened, never
questioned. Never touched
a corpse to say good-bye.
Is loved by all.

No Admittance

Out of the shadows
    Off the beaten track
        Across the avenue
            On the other side of town

Below the hidden magazines
    Behind the veil behind the veil
        To the source of silences
            In the other room

Between the mutilated pages
    Of the expurgated manuscript
        Stripped down to nothing
            Into forbidden arms

Without either of your lovers
    Within the echo of a kiss

Trailer Park Self-Portrait
Mobile, Alabama, 1983

Hmmm . . . I bet you're really
Straight . . . You're all man, he
whispers in the dark; *I bet*
you don't get fucked, he whispers
unbuttoning, unzipping; *I bet*
you have a big dick, he
whispers, reaching; *You like*
to fuck all night, he whispers,
salivating; *I bet I'd like*
to take it all night too . . . I
sure would like to try

I cannot see myself in his blue eyes

In the dark he whispers, *Sorry*
but you have to go; My
family you know, he whispers
buttoning, zipping; *They*
know, you know, he whispers,
reaching, *how I'm . . . guys . . . you*
know they're cool . . . but this . . . ,
he whispers, wiping up, *but you . . .*
a black man . . . you, in the dark
he whispers, *you*
they wouldn't understand;
Hmm . . . I don't even want to try

I cannot see myself in his blue eyes.

Magicians

After I got up this morning
to wipe your silken kisses from my body,

rinse your whispered lies out of my ears,
you showed me one last card trick

to end our time together
as it began.

I know one, too, I said,
taking the deck, shuffling:

This is called,
the disappearing hearts.

What Are You?

they ask me in Atlanta
dazzled by tight curls, fine-grained
"good hair." *You part Mexican,*
Spanish, South American,
from The Islands? You ain't all black.

My Scotch Irish ancestors snigger
from beneath my skin, inbreeding
"high-yella" forebears sigh in praise
song inside my breath, relieved,
believing their job well done.

Pero soy quien soy
Je suis africain
Esta escuridão está me
Ain't I still your nigga, yo?

Travel Journal

Memory of your
heartbeat pulsing in my hand:
all the windows open   Dawn

          The clocks here all face
          East   Time measured out
          in backward moving spoons
          empty as an unmade bed.

                    Your photograph haunts
                    the shifting room, thin
                    substitute for absent arms.
                    Three zeros on the door.

Lifeboat for a shipwrecked
heart, phone lines
taut between us   Only sound
your voice

          Noon: The postcard lies
          face front: Glittering skyline, clear
          waters. The perfect day
          reversed: Empty words
          quickly tossed   *Good Time*
          Lovely   *Don't worry*

                    Truth   a knife edge
                    between word and image
                    slicing skin   paper-
                    thin with longing

"Wore your undershirt;
Green apples drifted through
my clothes all day
then went out to a bar.

                          The only guy
          who looked at me looked like
          you."
                    "I think that means
                         Come Home"

                    Sunset behind the
                    mountain   Golden crown on bed
                    of coffee beans.   Night.

The Secret of Our Success

Dishes pile up
    And get washed
Laundry accumulates
    And gets done—eventually
Days become weeks
    Become months become
        years

Fall asleep
    And it's been a year
Turn over
    And it's been a decade
Wake up
    And it's half your life

The youth-filled thrill
    Unspools into routine
        Endless as aisles in grocery stores
Passions bank into embrace
    A look, a touch, the familiar
        The body as warm blanket in winter

Memory betrays:
    Juggling future, present, past
        <u>Was</u> there a *Before you met*?

Another summer, another birthday,
    Another anniversary, a New Year
        And your lives go on

The City Without You

I

Thunderstorm and early morning

Rain

Wind a drunken boarder
who's lost his keys, rattling the windows.

                                                            The wrong
                                            house.

II

Bustling streets continue
bustling. Shining towers continue to
be named. Traffic lights
continue lighting, treadmill red to
green:

The city, continuing.

III

"Settled"
the way a house is settled into its foundations

IV

streets continue
names continue
lights continue

V

Haunted by

damp rhyming
A hovering of wings
distant violins
An ancient buzz of bees
Honeysuckle bristling on the tongue

Bouquet of ashes worrying the nose

VI

Continue
Continue
Continue
Continue

VII

The Differed Music:
caress of whispers

weight of razored sleep

veiled glimpse of song

O sweetest rain
wash the night from me

VIII

Continue

con

tin
contain

con

tune
you

c

—
—
—
—

IX

Won't be fingers
Won't be heartbeat
Won't be sense
Won't be city
Won't be
Won't be
Won't be

Poem Based on a Line by Forman

"Young Black Question" by Ruth Forman

Who's to say this sidewalk's
solid   Who's to say this side-
walk's where to walk   Who
to say this side's

the side to walk   Who's
to say to walk   To walk who to
what side

Who's to say Who Is   To say
who is to say   Whose
side   Walk where
Who is

        Say Who

Out of Town

Everyone there reminds you of someone else—
that woman in the hotel bar's the girl
you sat next to in kindergarten, those people

across the street look like the couple with four
bikes you helped outside Walmart last Christmas.
The guy at the gas station always begging change

is here transformed into a banker; the bus driver,
your first disastrous blind date in school. Names
gather at the tip of the tongue, refusing to go farther.
Even you,

       you no longer look like yourself here,
but that other guy, that actor, singer, football player,
the priest who married your friend's sister. The hoodlum
everyone mistakes you for.

Walking dusk's quiet, rolled up streets,
you peer into glowing houses at set-for-dinner tables,
the backs of empty chairs, a flickering TV set
at the end of a long hall illuminated by long-held and -lost desires,
stare through the mirrored glass, searching for
the life you could have led.

The Spinning Song

Pantoum for Herbie Nichols

House Party Starting—
    Enter Rhythm Street:
        Love Is Proximity,
            Blue Chopsticks.

Enter Rhythm Street,
    Love, Gloom, Cash, Love.
        Blue Chopsticks,
            Infatuation Eyes.

Love, Gloom, Cash, Love
    Revelations:
        Infatuation Eyes
            Serenade.

Revelations:
    Crisp Day,
        Serenade
            Every Cloud.

Crisp Day
    Hangover Triangle,
        Every Cloud
            Argumentative.

Hangover Triangle,
    Sunday Stroll—
        Argumentative
            Wildflower.

Sunday Stroll—
    It Didn't Happen.
        Wildflower
            Beyond Recall

It Didn't Happen
    House Party Starting.
        Beyond Recall:
            Love Is Proximity.

Bluetopia

Perfect is the crossroads
filled with mirrors: lilac-scented
torch songs shot through with regret.
A twilit sky. A fading musk troubling the skin.
          Wednesday night's prayer meeting   *Thursday morning's sin*

Outline of two lips
drying on the cheek. Echo of a whisper
dissolving in the ear as slurred as the sea,
as if one held a conch to it, searching for a name.
          Last month's paycheck   *This month's bills*

Aching. The sharp slap of memory
some called love. This music now rising like
the moon trailing whiskey, sweat, and juke joints.
Fleshy curve of horizon, seductive as a dream.
          Every day's gray work song   *Yesterday's guitar*

Among the Players

Dupont Circle, Washington, D.C.

The city swirls around them like a thought.
Undisturbed grand masters of the streets
plotting, huddling over boards of black
and tan, moving plastic pieces with practiced ease.
A furtive web of hustlers smiling the smile
of those who know but do not tell, scanning
unsuspecting marks. Poker-playing poets sit beside them,
deep inside the music of the game, pulling
rhythms from the rise and fall of stakes,
the dance of knight and pawn, queen and sudden ace,
the wheeling race of traffic with the dark
and a lone jackhammer's stuttered final song.

Sunday Brunch

Eastern Shore continued:
       The sun is shining   this after
          noon   every shadow dangerous   in
                         Howard Johnson's lobby

calling out your name   to fellow travelers
       A seminar on time   and how   to slice   it   lemon
          wedges or two   three-minute eggs   where my parents met

Tell: Where are you headed? Show me off to town
      Is there butter on the table   any comics
          on the page   Any making their own days around the edges

Under the arcades   such desolation makes
       a better life   one becomes more conscious
          of the words   of the ways   of what one knows
                  and says   says what one

would have been so long ago   should have said
      for I am so in love and   so out of it   all melted
          into air   give the liar's kiss that says I love you

My name is on the wheat bread ration list (*one day only for us   the enslaved*)
      Shine like the moon   sufficient   for all the work
          that's done   and yet too much   the riches

of the earth   begging   destitute   a child
       Looks like you're writing a letter—would you like help?   Restore
          you to the years the locusts ate   orange juice and champagne
                    homemade jam

detritus of mornings   outside Cambridge
        Go Down Moses   *Say a prayer*   dregs in the cup
              rocks in my bed   ashes and the lure of meaning
                              Why, oh tell me, why don't we
                              go out?

Colonnade Shop, Havana

Based on a photograph in "Walker Evans: Havana 1933" (Pantheon, 1989)

On the street of promises, signs are
            everywhere: an itching palm means
                        money coming in. Rub your nose—

someone you know is talking
            about you *now*. In your dreams
                        take nothing from the dead

but if you hear a barking dog,
            turn and ask what message it has
                        for you. It will lick your ear

and whisper, revealing all
            it has learned behind the cafés
                        and lonely cinemas, decode
                        the mathematics of the street,

reveal for you alone where
            numbers go to play, the imperfect
                        form they take waiting for
                        some lucky one to add a final rhyme.

You—Sleeper! Visions of a dog
means today play 663.

Deya

I

In Deya, the streets were scrubbed with wind-borne sand wheeling from be-
yond the Southern Ocean. Everyone wore masks like holdup men in Westerns,
and hats, chapped hands frozen in the act of tipping, pulling down. We wore
our caps, baseball or Kangol hooding our eyes, strode the streets unbowed, cool
gangsters casing banks we were dead-set on knocking over to the furtive looks of
disbelieving natives. *Ve—Los negros,* they whispered into their upturned collars!
Ve te, Ve! (*They come, They come! Look, look!*), only mildly chiding children as they
pointed, strained to touch our hair, our skin, to see if this kinky nimbus, pitch-
black cloak of night would change under their thin white hands, suddenly rub
off. It never did.

II

After five straight hours I pulled over, let *him* drive, drifted into dreaming before
my eyes closed, feeling lips on mine, a familiar song, the long-promised kisses
I had not gotten in the morning. A lover's face. A black-clad band of brothers.
A dream lover's face, moving with imagination's too deliberate speed toward ca-
resses that never happened, never will. The ache of wanting salty in my mouth,
Tantalus's punishment to feel the longed-for oasis hovering just beyond the next
curve in the road, just around the bend, and never get there, like standing beside
some dark beloved, watching him luxuriate in another's arms. Waking with a
start, tears in my eyes as the other's face comes slowly clear. It is my own. *What
is it?* Deya asked. Blushing, my face parted, formed an enigmatic smile.

III

Wandering, fading light as slanted as a pitching boat in the middle of a storm,
the sky's electric, poised upon a precipice, in love with its impending fall, flash-
ing rays of sun thin knives slipped between the ribs of clouds. Rudderless, alone,

bruised as if beaten by betrayal, you stumble on, enraged, cold, in a fury without center, the winds angered by some distant slight, pure hatred turning inward on itself. The bare lonesomeness of walls seeps into you. Try to shake it off, stare into clouds brought low by thunder, the tops of buildings obscured from sight as if the center of the earth had suddenly caught fire. *There is a name for this time of day here,* the guidebooks tell you. *They call it Deya. It is better not to venture out.*

IV

Half-past lost. Or evenings of the days that drag forever onward, threatening not to end. The empty opening inside. Nights pitch-black with exhaustion, filled with graveyards and dark pits. Afterward, as bodies peel from one another, separate back to separate beings from an uninspired coupling, avoiding touch or eyes to mask faces filled with embarrassment, with shame. Homecomings to a silent room, air aswirl with the other's leaving, click of a suitcase quickly filled, rip of zippered bags still echoing down the hall. Or before. The open emptiness inside. Rise. Go to another room. Drink a glass of water slowly and relax. Fill the weeping lungs with air, try to speak. *Deya*—whisper softly. *Deya.*

New Rules of the Road

Make
    No sudden movements
        Like from your neighborhood
            To someplace you don't belong

Keep
    Your hands visible at all times
        Above your head   In these
            Brand new handcuffs

Speak
    Only when spoken to
        Or not at all   You have the right to
            Silence

Have proper ID on you at
    All times
        There is no right
            To travel

Reply only to
    The questions asked
        You have nothing to say
            We want to hear

Give the officer
    Only the materials requested
        You have nothing to show us
            We want to see

Do not leave the vehicle
    Unless told to
        You have
                Nothing

Go quietly
    When arrested
        You are
                Nothing

Do not
    Resist
        You are a
                Thing

Do not
    Run
        You have
                No rights

Do not say you
    Do not fit the profile

        This is America:
                You *are* the profile

On the Road

Dreamtime in Jasper, Texas

Imagine you wake up with
a second chance: Silent evening
wider than tomorrow, each breeze
a kiss from heaven. Tired out
from work, but you don't mind
the walk.   Still, an offered ride
is welcome.

At what point does the road narrow,
turn? When do the minds beside you
unmask themselves? Do their eyes reflect
white hoods before or after you are
beaten? Between the kicks? Before or
after you are chained to the
rust-pocked bumper?

If you don't look back the future
never happens: the road does not rise
to meet your broken body, the
last taste in your mouth is honeydew
not metal, blood, and fear.

Funny what the mind will focus on:
A silent calf standing in a field.
The blink of fireflies.
The way your leg twists back
onto itself. A dented license plate
the last thing of this world you see
as your head rips from your body.

Imagine you wake up with
a second chance.

Imagine
you wake up.

Captain Blackman

I slip into the line, the black men
of the Coast Guard cutter *Westwind*
on the way to officer's call on the docks in
Pascagoula, Mississippi.

We don't march but swagger, strut
distinctive bops from the cities of the
East and West, Midwest and South,
melding into one firm cadence

we were taught in boot camp,
distinctive *left-right-left* drilled
into us by black sergeants, most
blocked from rising further,

determined to mold us into something
bigger, better than ourselves,
to make us their own. Taught us
to march forward then drop
in reverse on a dime,

saunter off in the opposite direction
in formation, and not miss a step
astonishing outsiders.
Not much call for that now, it seems,
our ship in dry-dock in the South.

I step into the line,
        march back to Bunker Hill,
                the snows of Valley Forge,
                        the sunny plain of Yorktown

left   left   left-right-left

I step into the line,
       smoldering Atlanta at our backs
              Richmond in our eyes, blessing cheers
                     of the freed around us in our ears

left   left   left-right-left

I step into the line,
       chasing others as dark, darker
              than ourselves across the West
                     back onto the reservation

left   left   left-right-left

I step into the line,
       marching back from Paris
              into Harlem's teeming streets,
                     Europe's rhythm ringing in our ears

left   left   left-right-left

I step into the line,
       stomping Hitler, the Japanese,
              the freedom we were fighting for back
                     into the throats of white America

left   left   left-right-left

I step into the line,
       beside my uncle outside Pusan, both
              gay, we share laughs, cigarettes
                     and secrets only men like us know

right   left   right-left-right

I step into the line,
       help my paratrooper uncle
              into his harness, pray the jungle air will
                     leach him of his madness before he lands back home

left   left   left-right-left

I step into the line,
       reverse march through the
              looking glass of time to a swamp of sand,
                     cradle of civilization locked in shock and awe

left   left   left-right-left

We step into the line,
       march forward then reverse
              saunter, boots echoing down the docks
                     bigger, better, all our own.

left   left   left-right-left

Step into the line.

Retreat Postcards

I

Mass of granite   question mark
fear trapped in your suitcase

               r   e   l   e   a   s   e   d

forgotten with each embrace
repeated invocation
Welcome

II

Beloved:
Times are wonder-
filled.   You   here
my wish
to overflow them.

III

The ghosts are friendly here
helpful novices urging   joy
        depth   prayer.   Courage.

They fly in with a gust at night
to peer over your shoulder.

Messy haints:
try to catch them
they rearrange your pages as they flee.

IV

Mother:
I cried out for you, for God,
begged forgiveness staring at the stars,
was up all night suspended
in an envelope   slipped from dusk to dawn.
The feel of being cupped in loving hands,
sound of fifty heartbeats echoing—
How can I go on?

Prepare:
Visions are next

V

Block of foot-thick stone and prayer
light above the river.   Angels hovering
wings thin as pure blank pages.

Nom de Plume

The urge toward erasure:
    If you can't tear it
        down, mess it up.

Looking for a mirror
    give them paper, all
        surface, no reflection.

Tongue a clotted machine
    for making, telling it
        like it ain't.

A hole in my voice
    where a name might have been:
        Mythology of ever-changing objects.

Inscrutable blank space
    turning everything that enters
        Colored, impossible to see.

Haunted whisper
    troubling the ear.
        Same as your memory of me.

Marvin Gaye Sings "The Star-Spangled Banner"
NBA All-Star Game, February 13, 1983

This is about Love.   About Pain.
About how sweet it is,
the Real Thing.
                    Direct.
                              Unrequited.
                                        One-sided.
                                                            Can I get a witness?

But he's known "One More Heartache."
He knows all about that.

about love trapped in the blood   no getaway
even after you've gone:
Leave her,

                                                            My mistake

leave town,

                                                                  was to love you

the country.

                                                            When did you
                                                                  stop loving me . . . ?

Marvin sings.
      If this world were mine

He knows words can lie, conceal,

                                                            Heard it through
                                                                  the grapevine

makes this song a promissory note,
makes (Midnight) love to
The Dream

hushed, sensual,
slow healing.
His tribe Last of the Believers

Makes me wanna holler

the only Real Americans left

the way They do my life

yearning.

Marvin sings. Caresses words.
The nation, fickle,
seduced by the familiar:
a distant lover persuaded to do right

That's the way love is

gently

before she gives up her Secret,
releases Freedom,
a river, soft as her kiss

All I need to get by

then strong and sudden, true,
says *Let's Get It . . .*
with bombs bursting in air

Can I get a WIT-ness?

by Dawn's

Early

Light

(*Do you know the meaning of
"Been Sanctified"?*)

Packing

Gun on my lip
Thorn in my ear
Sun in my throat
Torch in my pants

Ass in a twist
Knife in my eye
Bone in my heart
Flame in my palm

Reginald Harris is the recipient of Individual Artist Awards for both poetry and fiction from the Maryland State Arts Council, a Pushcart Prize nominee, and a graduate of the Cave Canem: African American Poetry Workshop/Retreat. He serves as information technology director and coordinator of Poetry in The Branches at Poets House in New York City. His first book, *10 Tongues* (2001), was a finalist for a Lambda Literary Award and the ForeWord Book of the Year. His poetry, fiction, reviews, and articles have appeared in numerous journals and websites, including *African-American Review, Beltway, 5 AM, Gargoyle, Smartish Pace,* and *Sou'wester;* and in the anthologies *Best Gay Poetry 2008; Voices Rising: Celebrating 20 Years of Black Lesbian, Gay, Bisexual and Transgender Writing;* and *The Ringing Ear: Black Poets Lean South.*